GREAT 20TH CENTURY EXPEDITIONS

AMELIA EARHART FLIES AROUND THE WORLD

Kath Davies

Dillon Press
New York

First American publication 1994 by Dillon Press, Macmillan Publishing Company, 866 Third Avenue, New York, NY 10022

Macmillan Publishing Company is part of the Maxwell Communication Group of Companies.

First published in Great Britain by Zoë Books Limited.

A ZOË BOOK

Devised and produced by
Zoë Books Limited
15 Worthy Lane
Winchester
Hampshire SO23 7AB
England

Printed in Italy by Grafedit SpA
Design: Jan Sterling, Sterling Associates
Picture research: Faith Perkins
Illustrations and maps: Gecko Limited
Production: Grahame Griffiths

10 9 8 7 6 5 4 3 2 1

Library of Congress Cataloging-in-Publication Data

Davies, Kath.
  Amelia Earhart flies around the world / Kath Davies.
    p. cm. — (Great 20th century expeditions)
  Includes bibliographical references and index.
  ISBN 0-87518-531-2
    1. Air pilots—United States—Biography—Juvenile literature. 2. Earhart, Amelia, 1897-1937—Juvenile literature. [1. Earhart, Amelia, 1897-1937. 2. Air pilots.] I. Title. II. Series.
  TL540.E3D383 1994
  621.13'092—dc20
  [B]   93-29544

Summary: The story of Amelia Earhart's life, with special emphasis on her aviation career and flying expeditions around the world, ending with her mysterious disappearance in 1937.

Photographic acknowledgments

The publishers wish to acknowledge, with thanks, the following photographic sources:

Celtic Picture Library: 18; John Frost Historical Newspapers: 27; Hulton-Deutsch Collection: title, 5t, 8b, 10, 13t & b, 17, 19tl, 20, 21t, 23, 25b, 26b; Illustrated London News: 22; Peter Newark's Historical Pictures: 7t & b, 11t, 12, 15, 21b, 24l; Popperfoto: 5b, 16, 19b; The Royal Aeronautical Society: 9, 14b; The Schlesinger Library, Radcliffe College: 6, 11b, 14t, 29t; Topham Picture Source: 8t, 19tr, 24r, 25t, 26t, 28, 29b

Cover photographs courtesy of Roland Reynolds and the Hulton-Deutsch Collection

The publishers have made every effort to trace the copyright holders, but if they have inadvertently overlooked any, they will be pleased to make the necessary arrangement at the first opportunity.

Contents

Missing!

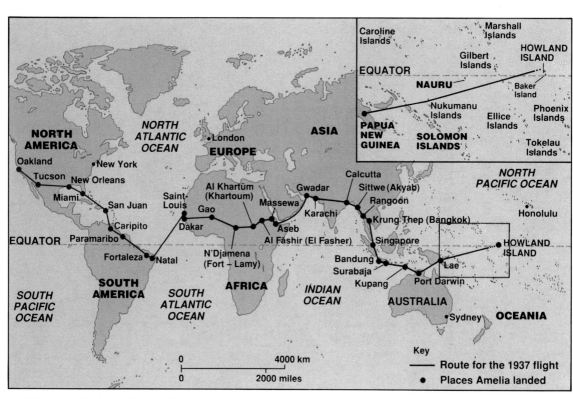

▲ The route for Amelia's last journey

July 2, 1937: The world waited for news of Amelia Earhart, missing on the last stages of her around-the-world flight. Amelia was attempting to fly from Lae in Papua New Guinea to Howland Island in the Pacific Ocean, where she would refuel her plane before flying on to California and home. Amelia had already flown 22,000 miles (32,000 kilometers) since the start of her journey on May 21. After Lae, she faced another 7,000 miles (11,000 kilometers), flying most of the time over the waters of the Pacific. The stop on Howland, which was about 2,550 miles (4,000 kilometers) from Lae, was vital.

It was the job of Fred Noonan, who flew with Amelia, to keep the plane on course for the island. Noonan was the **navigator**. He knew the area well, and had worked with Pan American Airways, **mapping** out routes across the Pacific. But Howland Island was only 2 miles (3 kilometers) wide and half a mile (three-quarters of a kilometer) long. It would take all his skill as a navigator, and Amelia's as a pilot, to make a safe landing there.

No signals

The American ship *Itasca*, a Coast Guard **cutter**, was near Howland Island, waiting to receive radio signals from Amelia. Captain Warner Thompson reported the

▲ Amelia Earhart standing by her plane

first signal at 2:45 A.M. For the next six hours, as Amelia flew closer, ship and plane tried to send and receive messages to guide Amelia and Noonan to Howland, but often the signals were too faint to hear properly. At 8:47 A.M the *Itasca* heard the last signal from Amelia. Then silence. The plane never arrived at Howland. No trace of it, or of Amelia and Noonan, has ever been found.

A huge search began almost immediately. It was ordered by the president of the United States, Franklin D. Roosevelt, himself. It is said to have cost more than $4.5 million. The American aircraft carrier *Lexington*, with other ships and 66 aircraft, combed an area of about 25,000 square miles (40,000 square kilometers). They found nothing.

A mystery

How did it happen? How could Amelia Earhart, a woman who had spent almost twenty years flying, and who knew the dangers very well, have been lost? She had flown the Atlantic **solo**—the first woman and only the second person to do so. She had **campaigned** about the safety of flying. She and Noonan were in one of the best-equipped private aircraft in the world, and Noonan was an experienced and skillful navigator. What went wrong?

Who was Amelia Earhart, and what made her risk her life so many times? She wrote, "I know the hazards," but no hazard kept her from what she called "the last great adventure." Did she really die in the Pacific in 1937? There are those people who say she did not. Here is the story of the woman whose last flight has become a legend.

▼ Amelia in England in 1932

The early years

Amelia Mary Earhart was born on July 24, 1897 in Atchison, Kansas. This town grew up more than 100 years ago because it was a good place for wagon trains to cross the Missouri River on their way to the American West. Amelia's **ancestors** were French, English, and German pioneers, and she seems to have inherited her courage and her adventurous spirit from them. Her mother, Amy, was the first woman to climb Pikes Peak in Colorado.

Hammer and nails

Amelia's early life was happy. Her father, Edwin Stanton Earhart, was a young lawyer who was beginning to make a name for himself. His work often took him away from home, when Amelia ("Millie") and her younger sister, Muriel ("Pidge"), would stay with their grandparents. Amelia's grandfather was a wealthy and well-known judge, Alfred Gideon Otis.

Amelia showed an early interest in travel —she made her doll carriage into a stagecoach! She also liked to spend time making things with hammer and nails. When she was only seven years old, she

▼ Amelia as a young girl

built her own roller coaster in the backyard.

Amelia's mother, unlike many mothers, decided to dress the girls in trousers instead of the frilly pinafores that most girls wore at that time. When she was nine years old, Amelia's father gave her a small rifle so that she could get rid of the rats in the barn! At school, Amelia was called "the girl in brown who walks alone." She knew what she wanted—a workshop where girls could learn to use motors, gadgets, and all types of mechanical things.

Sadly, Amelia's father was not successful in his career. He became an alcoholic, and he was never able to provide for the family properly. They lived in Kansas City and in Des Moines, Iowa, and sometimes they stayed again with her grandparents in Atchison, as their father moved from job to job. Finally, Amelia's mother took the two girls to live in Chicago, and their father returned to Kansas to look for work.

To Canada

Amelia's grandmother died in 1911, leaving money for the girls' education.

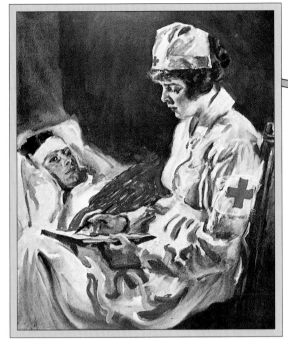

▲ Amelia worked as a nurse during World War I.

Muriel went to Toronto, to study to become a teacher. Amelia went to the Ogontz School in Philadelphia. At Christmas of 1917, she visited Muriel in Toronto. Canada, which was part of the British Empire, had been at war since 1914. The hospitals were full of wounded soldiers. Amelia decided to give up her studies and to work as a Voluntary Aid Detachment (VAD) nurse at the Spadina Military Convalescent Hospital in Toronto. She remained at the hospital until the end of the war in November 1918. It was at Spadina that Amelia became interested in flying. Amelia listened to the tales of the young flying officers in the hospital, and she visited the nearby military airfield at Armour Heights. She was not allowed to try flying herself, but she later said that she "hung around" the airfield, and "absorbed all I could." Later, Amelia said that the development of flying was one of the few good things to come out of World War I.

▼ War in the air, 1914–1918

Amelia's first flight

Nursing had completely exhausted
Amelia. She had bad headaches and pain
in her face. This sinusitis was to come
back whenever Amelia was tired or
anxious throughout her life. She also had
pneumonia. Her sister, Muriel, had moved
from Toronto to Northampton,

▶ Amelia as an undergraduate, 1918

▼ Amelia learns to fly

Massachusetts, to study. Amelia joined Muriel to rest and recover from her illness.

At Northampton Amelia decided to become a doctor, so she entered Columbia University in New York City. She studied **chemistry** and **biology**, and she was interested in poetry and music, playing the banjo in her spare time. She also climbed to the top of the dome of the university library!

To an air show

Amelia enjoyed her life as a student, but she had no clear idea of what she wanted to do with her life. She gave up the idea of becoming a doctor, and thought that she might do medical **research** instead. However, when her parents decided to live together again, in California, Amelia agreed to join them. She fully intended to return to her studies, but while she was in California, something happened that was to change the course of Amelia's life.

Amelia was always interested in what were known as "air circuses." These popular shows included flying displays and **stunts**. In California she went with her father to an air show at Long Beach, where flights were being offered to the public at $10 a journey.

Amelia booked a flight. Before she even went up, she asked her father to find out about the cost of flying lessons.

Takeoff!

The next day, Amelia flew for the first time. Her pilot was Frank Hawks, who would later become a record-breaking speed flyer. Amelia said she was surprised that she had so little sense of speed in the air, and that the engine was so noisy. She was also surprised because the ground looked so unfamiliar—but it was love at first flight! As soon as she was in the air, she knew that she had to fly. By the time she landed, she was determined to find the money for flying lessons.

Amelia's future, like the future of flying, was beginning to take shape.

▼ Frank Hawks, pilot on Amelia's first flight

Flying firsts

Amelia Earhart made her first flight in December 1920. It was less than 20 years since the first flight ever made by an aircraft with an engine. On December 17, 1903, Orville and Wilbur Wright's plane flew for 12 seconds at a height of 10 feet (3 meters) over a distance of 120 feet (37 meters) at Kitty Hawk, North Carolina. Only four years later, in 1907, the world's first airfield, an **aerodrome**, was opened in France. By that time, planes could fly distances of about 50 miles (80 kilometers), and interest in the new form of travel was growing throughout the world. In 1908, the first flying club, the Aeronautical Society of New York, was set up.

In 1909 the first flying show was held in France, and the Frenchman Louis Blériot

▲ The first powered flight, December 17, 1903

flew across the English Channel. French aircraft engineers built and tested the first **seaplane** in 1910. The British were the first to use planes for carrying mail, starting up an airmail service in 1911. The world's first passenger service carried people across Tampa Bay in Florida from 1914—but the plane could fly only one passenger on each trip!

Many people loved the excitement of flying. They soon began to try to break records, flying higher, lower, faster, or farther than anyone else. In 1912 the American Albert Berry became the first person to jump out of an aircraft using a parachute. This feat was repeated by a

▲ Stunt flying in the 1920s

woman, Georgina Broadwick, the following year.

Women in the air

Women as well as men were involved in the early days of flying. In 1908 Thérèse Peltier became the world's first woman passenger, flying over Turin in Italy. She was also the first woman to fly alone— making a solo flight. In England, Mabel Cody, an American, flew with her husband, the Wild West showman Buffalo Bill Cody, in 1910. In the United States, Mrs. Van Deman was one of Wilbur Wright's passengers in 1909. Inevitably, some of the first woman pilots were killed in flying accidents. Raymonde de Laroche of France and Edith Maud Cook, the first British woman to make a solo flight, both died.

The first American woman who is known to have flown alone was Blanche Stuart Scott. She was trained by Glenn Curtiss, who founded the first American aircraft company in 1907. Blanche Stuart Scott became a daring stunt flyer, diving under bridges and flying upside down. However, after a short but brilliant career, she retired because she felt that women were not taken seriously in flying.

The first woman pilot to be officially recognized in the United States was Bessica Medler. She was fascinated by Raymonde de Laroche's adventures in France, where she went to study music. On her return to the United States, Bessica and her husband built a small plane in their living room! Bessica made her first flight in this plane in 1910. She was called "the first woman **aviator** of America." In 1911 Harriet Quimby became the first American woman to receive a pilot's certificate, and in 1912 she was the first woman to fly the English Channel. Later that year, she was killed in a flying accident over Boston, Massachusetts.

▼ Amelia Earhart in the 1920s

War and peace

During World War I (1914–1918), aircraft became very important. They were used to gather information about the enemy, such as where their troops were or how many factories they had to make weapons. As well as this **reconnaissance** work, aircraft were used to drop bombs. They also fought in the air, attacking other planes. Countries such as Germany, Britain, Holland, Russia, and the United States all tried to make better and more efficient aircraft. They improved the shape of the wings and the size and weight of the

▼ Alcock and Whitten-Brown, first transatlantic fliers, 1919

engines. Instead of wood and silk, planes began to be made of metal. The coming of war meant that aircraft development happened much more quickly than it might otherwise have done.

By 1914 Britain had formed the Royal Flying Corps (RFC) and the Royal Naval Air Service (RNAS). Young men and women volunteered to join, but only men were allowed to fly. Both Britain and the United States refused to allow women to become pilots in their air services. Even women who were already pilots could not fly. Russia and France, however, did not ban women from flying in their air forces. It seems strange now that women who were not allowed to fly for their country had actually trained some of the first young men to be pilots! In Britain, Hilda Hewlett trained fighter pilots, in Germany Melli Beese ran a flying school, and in the United States Katherine and Marjorie Stinson owned an aircraft company and ran a training school. Even Ruth Law, a pilot and stunt flier, was refused by the American armed forces.

Atlantic fliers

After the war, many of the planes that had been used in the air forces were no longer needed. People who were interested in flying were able to buy them. Flying became more and more popular. In 1919 two British fliers, John Alcock and Arthur Whitten-Brown, flew across the Atlantic Ocean. It took them 16 hours and 27 minutes to fly from Newfoundland to

▲ Lindbergh and the *Spirit of St. Louis*, 1927

Ireland in their Vickers Vimy bomber.

This "first" was to be followed by Charles Lindbergh's solo crossing of the Atlantic in May 1927. The excitement of Alcock and Whitten-Brown's first transatlantic flight had led a Frenchman, Raymond Orteig, to offer a prize for the first person who could fly the Atlantic alone. The prize was to be $25,000, and the distance, from the

United States to France, 3,600 miles (5,600 kilometers), was almost twice as far as Alcock and Whitten-Brown had flown.

Charles Lindbergh was only 25 years old when he made his record-breaking flight. He had been a stunt pilot and had flown with the U.S. Mail service. He flew across the Atlantic without a radio or a **fuel gauge**, at an average speed of 107.5 mph (172 kilometers per hour). About 100,000 people welcomed him when he landed at Le Bourget Airport, Paris, on May 21. Lindbergh sailed back to the United States on a navy warship by command of the president, and was given the Medal of Honor, the United States' highest military honor. Five years later, Amelia Earhart was to receive a similar welcome, when she made her own flight across the Atlantic.

▼ Amelia Earhart and Charles Lindbergh looked so much alike that Amelia was often called "Lady Lindy."

One of the best

Amelia's parents did not object to her learning to fly, but they could not afford to pay for her lessons. So she decided to get a job to pay for the lessons herself. Amelia would never be put off once she had decided to do something. She believed that one day flying would be as common as taking the train. She also believed that women should take part in the future of flying.

She took flying lessons from Anita "Neta" Snook, a woman pilot who was as determined as Amelia was that women should fly. Neta worked at the Kinner airfield in California, which was owned by Bill Kinner, a designer and builder of aircraft. After only a few hours of lessons, Amelia, helped by her mother, bought her

▲ Amelia (on the right) and her flying teacher, Anita "Neta" Snook
▼ Bill Kinner, aircraft designer

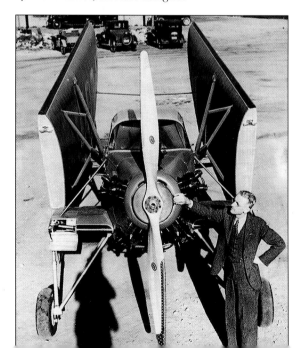

▲ A poster from the 1920s

first plane. It was a Kinner sports plane, the Airster. Amelia called it the *Canary* because it was painted bright yellow. The aircraft had a 60-horsepower, air-cooled engine and it was so light that Amelia could pick it up by the tail and move it without help!

Amelia goes solo

During the years following her first flight, Amelia spent all her free time at the Long Beach Boulevard airfield. She and Neta dressed like other pilots, in long boots, leather jacket, and riding breeches. Amelia deliberately roughened a leather coat so that it would not look too new! In 1922 Amelia made her first solo flight—and immediately broke the height record for women's flying. She flew at 14,000 feet (4,267 meters). This record was in turn broken by another woman, Ruth Nichols, a few weeks later. Amelia then tried to beat Ruth's record—and crashed. To Amelia, as to other fliers of the time, bumps and crashes were all part of flying. As well as her first job with a telephone company, Amelia said later that she had taken 28 jobs to pay for her flying. Among these were driving a truck, selling sausages, and processing photographic film. She was quite determined to continue flying. At this time her parents' marriage was breaking down again, and in 1924 they divorced. Amelia sold her plane to a young man who instantly killed himself in it, stunt flying. She bought a yellow touring car, her "yellow peril," and drove her mother across the United States to see Muriel, who was living on the East Coast.

The flying teacher

In Boston, Amelia had an operation for her sinusitis and then took up her medical studies again. After a time she dropped out of these, and became a social worker at Denison House in Boston. Her job was to teach English to immigrant families, and it was work that Amelia loved. At the same time, she kept up her flying. By 1927 Amelia had more than 500 hours flying experience and was becoming well known in the flying world. The Boston *Globe* called her one of "the best woman pilots in the United States."

Amelia might have gone on working at Denison House, flying when she could afford to, and marrying the young man, Sam Chapman, to whom she had become engaged. But in April 1927, she received a telephone call that was to change her life.

A "shining adventure"

Amelia's 1927 telephone call was from a Captain H. H. Railey. He spoke of an exciting flying project, in which he thought she would be interested. When they met to discuss it, Captain Railey said that an expedition was already being planned. He invited Amelia to join, saying, "How would you like to be the first woman to fly the Atlantic?"

The Atlantic Ocean was one of the great obstacles to international flying. It had been flown only six times since Alcock and Whitten-Brown's flight in 1919, including Lindbergh's famous crossing. Already in 1927 nineteen people had died trying to fly across, and three women had failed to become the first to cross as passengers. The British-born Princess Ann Loewenstein-Wertheim and Frances

▼ Captain Richard Byrd and his flying team

Grayson of the United States had been killed. The American flier Ruth Elder had been rescued. Only a month before Amelia's invitation, a British woman, the Honorable Elsie Mackay, and her pilot were also lost. Amelia knew that she would be risking her life on this expedition.

Fitting out the *Friendship*

The expedition that Amelia was to join was organized and paid for by Amy Guest. Amy Guest was a wealthy American whose English husband had been British secretary of state for air, from 1921–1922. Amy Guest wanted to fly herself, but her family made such a fuss that she finally gave up the idea. Instead, she looked for someone to take her place. Amelia had been suggested by a Rear Admiral Belknap, who knew of her flying record. In spite of the dangers, Amelia said, "How could I refuse such a shining adventure?"

Amy Guest had acquired a three-engined Fokker plane for the flight across the Atlantic Ocean. The plane had belonged to Captain Richard Byrd, leader of the flying expedition over the South Pole. She called the aircraft *Friendship*, to show goodwill between the United States and Britain. It was carefully adapted for the long flight. There were two extra fuel tanks on the wings, each holding about 95 gallons (360 liters) of fuel. In the body of the plane, the **fuselage**, were another two tanks, each holding about 245 gallons (927 liters) of fuel. Each of the three engines was 220 horsepower, and the

aircraft was fitted with light floats, not wheels, for landing on water. Its wing span was 72 feet (22 meters) and it was painted bright orange.

Secret plans

Wilmer "Bill" Stultz was both pilot and navigator for the trip, and Louis Gordon was the **mechanic**. Both men were very experienced in flying. Another well-known pilot, Lewes Gower, was to be on board in case anything went wrong. Unfortunately, Gower had to be left behind when the plane had difficulty taking off because of

▲ Amelia at the door of the *Friendship*

the extra weight. Throughout all the preparations—checking instruments, working out the best route, watching weather conditions—the team kept the expedition secret. Other unsuccessful flights had been well publicized. This time George Palmer Putnam, an explorer and **publisher** who was interested in the flight and who was working with the team, decided that secrecy was best, until the expedition was in the air.

▼ The route for Amelia's first transatlantic flight

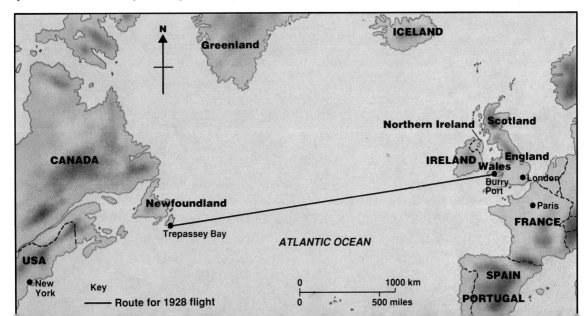

"20 hours 40 min"

▲ Burry Port, South Wales

On June 3, 1928, the *Friendship* took off from Boston, on its way to Trepassy Bay in Newfoundland. From there the route led east, and the team hoped to land in Ireland. As soon as they left Boston, George Putnam called a press conference to announce the trip to the world. The newspapers wrote, "Boston Woman Flies Into Dawn on Surprise Atlantic Trip."

In Newfoundland, bad weather delayed the flight for two weeks, and some changes had to be made to the plane. The team spent the time weather watching and plotting their route on their chart of the North Atlantic. Several times they lightened the plane by pumping out fuel. At last, on June 17, the weather seemed fair. After two failed attempts to take off, they ditched more fuel. Now they had only 700 gallons (2,650 liters). It was much more difficult to take off from sea than land, but after another false start, the *Friendship* finally rose into the skies.

Fog and storms

Amelia had never flown the plane before and she had no experience of flying in fog or clouds using only **instruments**. Even so, she was the commander of the expedition. She hoped to pilot the plane herself if weather conditions were good, but they were not. For most of the flight, Amelia sat on the extra clothing packed

▲ The *Friendship* on Southampton Water in 1928

▲ The welcoming committee, including Amy Guest and the mayor of Southampton

between the fuel tanks. Cushions had been left behind to cut down on weight. Amelia kept the journal, or **log**, of the flight. She noted down details of fog and storms—and when her ears hurt! As they used up the fuel they flew higher, wearing fur-lined suits as it became colder. All they had with them were sandwiches, coffee, and some oranges.

The weather was foggy and rough all through the night, and in the morning their radio was dead. They were running out of fuel and there was no sight of land. About half an hour later they saw fishing boats and landed in a sheltered bay. They had missed Ireland in the fog and landed at Burry Port in South Wales! The journey had taken 20 hours and 40 minutes, and this was to be the title of Amelia's later book.

Amelia becomes famous

The next day they flew on to a grand reception at Southampton, England. Amy Guest was there, with the mayor and many other important people. The press flocked around Amelia. She did not want all the attention, but no one was interested in the two men—a woman had flown the Atlantic for the first time!

A two-week whirl of activity followed. Amelia called it, "teas, theaters, speech-making, tennis, polo, and parliament." Even though Amelia, the passenger, said she had been as much use "as a sack of potatoes" on the flight, all the world wanted to see her. She was taken to shop at Selfridges, the great London store (she never traveled with even a nightdress!) and she visited Toynbee Hall, where social work similar to her own at Denison House was carried out.

▼ Amelia at Toynbee Hall, London, after her transatlantic flight

A heroine at home

Amelia received a heroine's welcome on her return to the United States. Huge crowds came out to give her a **ticker tape** parade in New York, and Boston and Chicago honored her, too. These events, and increasingly, Amelia's life, began to be organized by George Palmer Putnam. Amelia completed her account of the flight, which Putnam published, and she toured the United States, giving lectures about her "20 Hours 40 Min" over the Atlantic. She earned around $50,000 in the first few months after her flight, and of course she used the money to pay for her flying activities. She also helped her mother and sister with their living expenses.

Amelia was now able to fulfill some of her serious aims. She wanted more people to understand that flying was a safe form of travel. She also wanted them to accept, as she did, that women should play a part in the development of flying. Amelia became a **spokeswoman** for both these ideas. She sometimes lectured up to 27 different places in a month.

Amelia at work

Many offers of work flooded in for Amelia. She was amused that her flight seemed to make people think that she could do anything, from being a banker to an advertising manager. She did, however, write articles for magazines such as *Cosmopolitan*. The subjects were "What Miss Earhart Thinks When She Is Flying" or "Shall You Let Your Daughter Fly?" Amelia wanted everyone, and particularly young women, to consider flying as a career. She herself worked for Transcontinental Air Travel (which later became Trans World Airlines—TWA), making special flights to create interest in passenger services.

▼ Celebrating Amelia's homecoming in 1928

▲ Amelia posing for photographers

While in England, Amelia had bought a plane, an Avro Avian, from Lady Heath. Mary Heath had flown solo in the plane from South Africa to Britain, and she and Amelia became friends. Now Amelia decided to fly to California in the Avro Avian, to see her father and to attend the National Air Races. Her solo flight from Pittsburgh, Pennsylvania, was a new first. It was difficult, because there were no marked airfields. Once, her map blew out of the **cockpit**, and she had to land in the main street of a small town to find out where she was! She later campaigned for **aerial** markings to help pilots.

Throughout this time, George Putnam was working to keep Amelia in the public eye. He arranged lecture tours and personal appearances all over the country. Other women pilots were as experienced as Amelia and it was said that some of them were better fliers. But they had no one like George Putnam to work with them. Women such as Ruth Nichols, Louise Thaden, Ruth Elder, and Elinor Smith were all record-breaking pilots, yet they never received the same publicity.

New challenges

In 1929 Amelia worked at two special projects. With some of the other women pilots, she founded an organization of women fliers called the 99s Club. She also competed in the first Women's Air Derby—a race from Los Angeles to Cleveland, Ohio, which she helped to organize. Amelia flew a new plane, a Lockheed Vega, and although she led for part of the race, she came in third. Louise Thaden was the winner. Amelia broke the women's speed record in 1929, too, but still she felt that her reputation was perhaps not yet earned. What would she do next?

▼ National Air Race poster

Together and alone

THE FIRST WOMAN TO FLY THE ATLANTIC MARRIES A MEMBER OF A FAMOUS PUBLISHING FIRM AT NOANK, CONNECTICUT: MISS AMELIA EARHART AND MR. GEORGE PUTNAM.

▲ Amelia's wedding is announced in the *Illustrated London News*, February 21, 1931

In 1930 Amelia finally agreed to marry George Putnam. She had broken off her engagement to Sam Chapman some years before, and George was now divorced from his wife, Dorothy. Amelia and George had come to know each other very well over the years. They were married on Saturday, February 7, 1931, very quietly and secretly, at George's mother's house in Connecticut. Amelia wore her favorite color—brown—and no hat.

Before they were married, they had agreed that they would never try to stop each other from doing anything in "work or play," and they would not let the world see when they were either very happy or very sad. Amelia was always a private and rather shy person. They also agreed that if the marriage did not work, they would separate after a year.

Amelia and George were so busy that they did not have time for a honeymoon. George had given up his publishing work to manage Amelia's career full-time. Amelia, among other things, was flying for the Beech-Nut Company, to **promote** both an aircraft, the early type of helicopter called an **autogyro**, and the chewing gum made by Beech-Nut. She continued to break more records, flying to a height of 19,000 feet (5,790 meters) in the autogyro. She also wrote a new book about flying, called *The Fun of It*. About this time, a new idea was growing in

▲ Amelia at the controls of her Lockheed Vega

Amelia's mind—to fly the Atlantic solo. Amelia wanted to prove that she could do it, and she knew that other women were keen to try. Elinor Smith was also preparing for the flight. Amelia and George invited Bernt Balchen, a Norwegian pilot who had worked with Roald Amundsen and Richard Byrd on polar expeditions, to help them to prepare for the flight.

Going solo

Amelia's Lockheed Vega plane was specially adapted for the flight. A new 500-horse-power engine was fitted, and the body was strengthened to carry more fuel tanks. The flight would be more than 3,000 miles (4,800 kilometers), and the plane would have to carry about 420 gallons (1,590 liters) of fuel. New flying instruments were also fitted, including two **compasses** and a **drift indicator** to help Amelia to keep on course.

No one had flown the Atlantic solo since Charles Lindbergh in 1927. Amelia hoped to set off five years to the day after him, but she would not take the same route. She planned to fly from Harbour Grace, Newfoundland, aiming first for Britain, then Paris, France. As soon as the plane was ready, Amelia practiced flying "blind," using only instruments, and studied weather charts carefully. Seven women had already died trying to fly the Atlantic. Amelia asked Balchen, "Do you think I can make it?" and Balchen replied, "You bet."

▼ Amelia's planned route and the actual route on her solo transatlantic flight, 1932

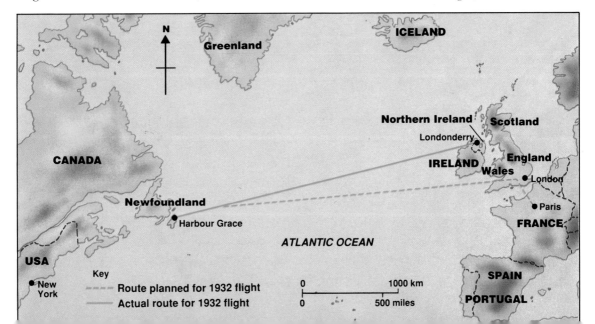

The Atlantic–solo

At 6:30 P.M. on the evening of May 20, 1932, Amelia took off from Harbour Grace, Newfoundland. At first, all was well —she later spoke of the beauty of flying in the moonlight.

Then things began to go wrong. The machine that showed her height, the **altimeter**, failed. There was an electrical storm, and the wings iced up. The plane fell almost 3,000 feet (1,000 meters) before it came out of its spin. Amelia also saw flames coming out of the **exhaust**.

Flying at about 10,000 feet (3,000 meters) into the morning light, Amelia knew she was low on fuel. Turning on the reserve tank, she discovered it was leaking, and there was a real danger of fire.

As soon as she saw land, Amelia decided to bring the plane down. She flew over a

▼ Amelia with the British flier Amy Johnson

THE FIRST WOMAN TO FLY THE ATLANTIC ALONE: MISS AMELIA EARHART AND HER 'PLANE AT CULMORE, NEAR LONDONDERRY, WHERE SHE WAS FORCED TO LAND.

▲ "In Gallegher's pasture"—Amelia lands in Northern Ireland.

town and landed in a large field. One farm worker and some cows were the only **witnesses**. "Where am I?" she asked the man, who replied, "In Gallegher's pasture" —she had landed in Northern Ireland. The journey had taken 14 hours and 54 minutes. Amelia had eaten nothing during the flight and she had drunk only one small can of tomato juice!

Amelia broke at least three records that day. Her flight was the first transatlantic crossing by a woman pilot. It was the first solo crossing by a woman, and it was the fastest crossing by anyone.

▲ Amelia receives a medal from the Society of Women Geographers.

Star of the skies

Crowds soon gathered as the news spread. Amelia spent the night with a nearby family, and flew to England the next day. Once again she was given star treatment. There were public appearances, dinners, and speeches. Again Amelia had to borrow clothes, since she had taken none with her. She met Britain's ace woman flier, Amy Johnson, who became a friend, and she danced with the Prince of Wales. Her Lockheed Vega was put on display in Selfridges' store. George Putnam joined her, and they traveled to Paris, Rome, and Brussels. Amelia met Pope Pius XI, the Italian dictator Benito Mussolini, and the king and queen of Belgium. She returned by sea to the United States again to a heroine's welcome.

As well as the honors that had been given to Amelia in Europe, she was now presented with the National Geographic Society's Gold Medal—the first woman to receive it. She dined at the White House with President Herbert and Mrs. Hoover, and she was awarded the Distinguished Flying Cross. She was specially pleased to receive the National Aeronautical Association's Honorary Membership. Only 14 men had already become members. She was the first woman to be made a member.

George Putnam became interested in movies, and began to work for Paramount Studios. Amelia considered making a film with the star Mary Pickford, but instead she continued her flying career. She broke more records, for a nonstop flight across the United States, and a flight from Hawaii to the North American mainland. She also joined Purdue University as careers adviser to women students, and went into business with charter airline owner Paul Mantz. Five busy years passed —until Amelia had an idea for "just one more long flight."

▼ President Hoover presents Amelia with the Gold Medal of the National Geographic Society.

The "last great adventure"

▲ Amelia inside her specially adapted Lockheed Electra, the "flying laboratory"

Amelia's work as an adviser to aircraft companies, flying schools, and to Purdue University's **aeronautical** department meant that she was becoming more interested in the **technical** areas of flying. In 1935 a group of wealthy people formed the Amelia Earhart Fund for Aeronautical Research. It aimed to buy and equip a "flying **laboratory**" that Amelia would fly. Two years later, Amelia piloted this aircraft on her "last great adventure," a bid to fly around the world.

Amelia wanted to make this flight for her own sake. If she succeeded, she would be the first woman to fly around the world. She also wanted to take part in the **scientific** work that the trip would involve. She would make notes on the effect of such a long flight on the mind and body of the fliers. She would research airfield provision across the world, and would test the instruments in the aircraft. Preparations for the flight took about two years, and as always, they were kept very secret.

Planning the expedition

Amelia's "flying laboratory" was a Lockheed Electra Model 10E, with two Pratt and Whitney WASP S3H-1 engines of 550 horsepower. It was the most up-to-date aircraft, and could fly at up to 27,000 feet (8,230 meters) at 210 miles (335 kilometers) per hour. It could travel 4,500 miles (7,200 kilometers) nonstop. There were extra fuel tanks, and the latest radio equipment and direction finder.

▼ Amelia flying over Golden Gate Bridge, San Francisco, on her first around-the-world attempt

While Amelia practiced flying the plane with the help of her technical adviser Paul Mantz, George Putnam organized the flight. He made arrangements for **visas** to other countries, for fuel stops, and for charts of the route to be bought—where they existed. The U.S. Navy agreed to help in the Pacific, and even President Roosevelt became involved. Amelia said of her flight that it would "produce practical results for the future of **commercial** flying, and for the women who may want to fly tomorrow's planes."

Setback and start

The first attempt ended in a crash at Honolulu. Instead of flying east-west, a new route, west-east, was planned. On June 1, 1937, Amelia and Fred Noonan left Miami and the United States behind.

All went well, and Amelia sent back reports as planned. Brazil was "just where it should be" and the Red Sea "was as blue as any other." At the fuel stops, Amelia impressed the mechanics who worked on the plane, when she worked alongside them "like a greased monkey."

By the end of June, Amelia and Fred Noonan had crossed the **equator** three times and landed 22 times. They were not intending to break speed records and were flying around the equator—the longest possible route. Amelia called it "a **leisurely** trip." They were able to send back valuable information about the plane's performance, about the accuracy (or not) of their maps and charts, and about the quality of airstrips on their journey. When they left Lae in Papua New Guinea they hoped to be back in the United States for Independence Day on July 4, but they were never seen again.

▼ Headlines from the *Chicago Herald and Examiner*

"Unless we dare"

The mystery of Amelia Earhart's disappearance has never been solved, although many people are still interested in what happened on that last flight. At the time, many **experts** gave opinions while the searching continued. Paul Mantz thought that the chances of landing on the sea and staying afloat were 1 in 1,000. Lockheed, however, said that the fuel tanks would keep the plane afloat for up to nine hours.

Amelia's friend Jacqueline Cochran, also an aviator, was sure that Amelia and Fred Noonan were alive, though injured, and drifting in the sea. Jacqueline claimed that she could "see" things—she was a **clairvoyant**. She said that a Japanese fishing boat was in the area. Two days later, she sensed that Amelia was dead.

Puzzles and theories

Other people have been certain that Amelia and Noonan were picked up by the Japanese. Many people thought that the real purpose of the flight was a spy mission for the American government. Three years after the expedition Japan was at war with the United States. Several people claimed to have seen Amelia, or Noonan, or both, on islands in the Pacific, or held captive by the Japanese. These sightings have since been disproved. Many, many years later, someone in the United States claimed to have met Amelia Earhart when she was a very old woman.

There was some criticism of Amelia's

▲ George Putnam with his son (left) and Paul Mantz—no news after weeks of searching for Amelia

flying on this last trip. She left behind one important piece of radio equipment, an aerial, and also the flares with which to signal for help. Other strange mistakes seem to have been made—for instance, why did she not know about a special direction finder on Howland Island, which she could have contacted by radio? Why did she not use some radio bands, or frequencies, that were available? Both Amelia and Fred Noonan were well aware of the importance of radio contact.

Whatever the manner of Amelia's death, her life and work were an inspiration to generations of young fliers. She showed the way for many young women to take up careers in flying—she was *the* "new woman" of her age, who by her independent life worked for women's

▲ Memorial stone to Amelia, Howland Island

rights and showed that she was the equal of anyone, man or woman. Amelia believed, as she said in one of the poems she wrote, that nothing would be won, "unless we dare."

Before her last flight she wrote, "Women should do for themselves what men have already done . . . and what men have not done, both for themselves and to encourage others." She also said, "Please know that I am quite aware of the hazards. I want to do it because I want to do it. Women must try to do things as men have tried. When they fail, their failure must be but a challenge to others."

For the last fifty-five years, from the first aviators to the late twentieth-century astronauts, young women and men have been taking up Amelia Earhart's challenge.

▼ Amelia at the U.S. embassy in London, with British fliers (seated, Mrs. Victor Bruce, Amelia, Mrs. Spencer Cleaver, standing, left, Lady Bailey, center, Peggy Salaman)

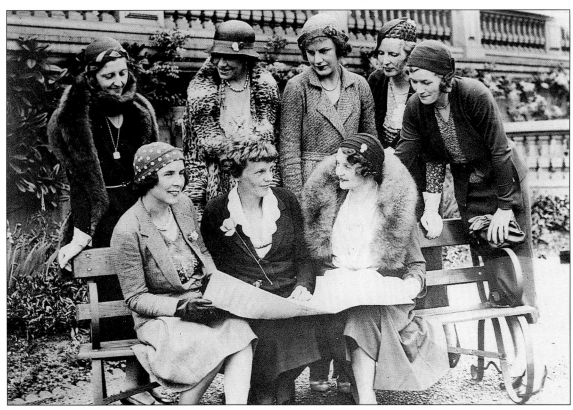

Glossary

aerial:	of the air
aerodrome:	large airfield, where aircraft land and take off, and where they are repaired
aeronautical:	to do with finding direction when flying
altimeter:	a machine for measuring the altitude of an aircraft
ancestors:	members of the family who died long ago
autogyro:	an early version of the helicopter, invented in Spain in 1923. A plane was fitted with rotor blades turned by airflow.
aviator:	a flier
biology:	the study of plants and animals
campaigning:	working very hard to make people aware of the need for change
chemistry:	the study of the materials or substances out of which things are made, and how they work together
clairvoyant:	a person who "sees" things that others cannot see, including future events
cockpit:	the part of an aircraft where the pilot sits
commercial:	to do with business—buying and selling
compass:	an instrument used for finding direction and position
cutter:	a small fast ship used by coast guards or customs officers
drift indicator:	an instrument for measuring how level an aircraft is flying—it measures the tilt of the wings
equator:	the imaginary line around the center of the earth
exhaust:	the pipe where gases from the aircraft engine can escape into the air
experts:	people who have studied a subject in detail and know a great deal about it
fuel gauge:	an instrument for measuring how much fuel is left in the fuel tank
fuselage:	the central framework of an aircraft
instruments:	machines that measure very accurately
laboratory:	a place where people carry out research and experiments
leisurely:	without hurrying

log:	an event-by-event record of a ship's voyage or of a flight
mapping:	making a drawing or chart of a route
mechanic:	a person who looks after machines and knows how they work, so that she or he is able to repair them
navigator:	a person whose job is to plot a course, and to keep to it, by air or sea
promote:	to speak or write well about something, in order to persuade people to buy it or to support it
publisher:	a person who works in the book trade. He or she arranges for books to be written, printed, and sold.
reconnaissance:	finding out about something
research:	a way of finding out—usually by scientific study and experiment
scientific:	a way of studying that involves organizing information carefully
seaplane:	an aircraft fitted with floats for landing on water
solo:	alone
spokeswoman:	a woman who is speaking on behalf of other people as well as herself
stunts:	daring or trick displays of flying
technical:	having a special skill or craft
ticker tape:	reels of thin paper on which telegraph messages were received. They were thrown from office windows onto a parade in the street below.
visa:	a document giving permission to visit a foreign country
witness:	someone who watches something happen

Further Reading

Kerby, Mona. *Amelia Earhart: Courage in the Sky*. New York: Viking Children's Books, 1990.

Larsen, Anita. *Amelia Earhart: Missing, Declared Dead*. New York: Crestwood House, 1992.

Lauber, Patricia. *Lost Star: The Story of Amelia Earhart*. New York: Scholastic, 1988.

Leder, Jane. *Amelia Earhart: Opposing Viewpoints*. San Diego, Cal.: Greenhaven Press, 1989.

Randolph, Blythe. *Amelia Earhart*. New York: Franklin Watts, 1987.

Tames, Richard. *Amelia Earhart*. New York: Franklin Watts, 1991.

Index

E DUE